Odd One Out

VEHICLES

Alix Wood

WINDMILL BOOKS

Published in 2023 by Windmill Books,
an Imprint of Rosen Publishing
2544 Clinton St.
Buffalo, NY 14224

Produced for Rosen Publishing by Alix Wood Books
Designed by Alix Wood
Edited by Eloise Macgregor
Editor for Rosen: Kerri O'Donnell

Photo credits:
All images © Shutterstock; or in the public domain, with grateful thanks to the photographers who allowed them to be creative commons

Printed in the United States of America

CPSIA Compliance Information: Batch CWWM23
For Further Information contact Rosen Publishing at 1-800-237-9932

Cataloging-in-Publication Data

Names: Wood, Alix.
Title: Vehicles/ Alix Wood.
Description: New York : Windmill Books, 2023. | Series: Odd one out | Includes answer key.
Identifiers: ISBN 9781538392645 (pbk) | ISBN 9781538392652 (library bound) | ISBN 9781538392669 (ebook)
Subjects: LCSH: Flying machines-- Juvenile literature | Vehicles-- Juvenile literature
Classification: LCC TL147 W66 2023 | DDC 629.04--dc23

Find us on

Can you find the odd one out? It's not always that easy!

The answers are on page 24

Which one is not ...

C-482BKY

a bus?

9
Trafalgar Square
Piccadilly Circus
Hyde Park Corner
ROYAL ALBERT HALL

Which vehicle is not ...

a digger or bulldozer?

Which is not ...

a motorcycle?

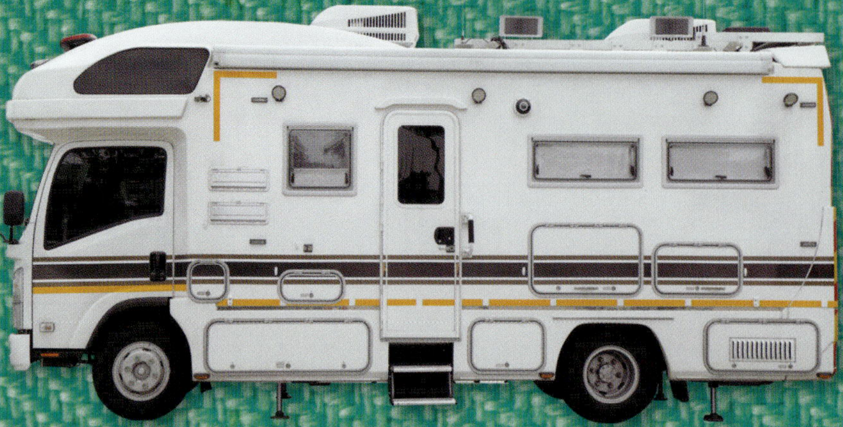

Which isn't ...

a motor home?

Can you see what ...

is not a balloon?

Which is not a train?

C 5615

One of these is ...

not an airplane.

Which vehicle is not ...

a truck?

Find what isn't ...

a helicopter.

Did you find the Odd One Out?

p 8-9

p 16-17

p 10-11

p 18-19

p 4-5

p 20-21

p 12-13

p 6-7

p 14-15

p 22-23